# MIRACULOUS

How Spiritual Awakening Cured My Depression,
Inspired My Purpose,
and Ignited the Intuitive Powers Within

Other books by Anne Deidre:

*Extreme Intuitive Makeover: 55 Keys to Health, Wealth & Happiness*

Forthcoming:
*Inner Circle Chronicles—Book One*

# MIRACULOUS

How Spiritual Awakening Cured My Depression,
Inspired My Purpose,
and Ignited the Intuitive Powers Within

## Anne Deidre

*Dear Ann, a message of We are already Enlightened as The painting Sunrise, new beginnings, circle of energy, transformation, Circle of friends, Circle of influence is expanding for you are expansion Itself + unlimited. Love & Blessings Anne*

Copyright © 2013 by Anne Deidre.
All rights reserved.

Published by
Radiant Heart Press
A division of HenschelHAUS Publishing, Inc.
2625 S. Greeley St. Suite 201
Milwaukee, WI 53207
www.HenschelHAUSbooks.com

ISBN: 978159598-225-4
e-ISBN: 978159598-226-1
LCCN: 2013935583

Printed in the United States of America.

*This book is dedicated to God and the voice of God within,
which is always with me, guiding in every moment.*

*It is also dedicated to my sons, Jacob and Brandon.
May they always be guided by their true selves
and know God within them, always.*

# THE STORY

This book has two parts. It is the story of the miracles that have happened in my life since a dark night of the soul led to a spiritual awakening and was followed by the messages of my Divinely inspired artwork.

I had suffered with depression and anxiety for most of my life, beginning in my late teens. It culminated in a debilitating depression I now recognize as a "Dark Night of the Soul." A dark night of the soul is described as a lengthy and profound absence of light and hope. It also precedes a profound illumination and deep connection with Higher Consciousness.

A poem by Saint John of the Cross narrates the journey of the soul from its bodily home to its union with God. The text was written in 1578 or 1579, while John of the Cross was imprisoned by his Carmelite brothers, who opposed his reformations to the Order. The journey is called "The Dark Night," because darkness represents the hardships and difficulties the soul meets in detachment from the world and reaching the light of the union with the Creator. The main idea of the poem can be seen as the painful experience that people endure as they seek to grow in spiritual maturity and union with God. The poem reflects the two phases of the dark night, with the first being a purification of the senses, the second and more intense is the purification of the spirit, which is the less common of the two. The term "Dark Night of the Soul" may also describe the ten steps on the ladder of mystical love.

In Christianity, the term "dark night (of the soul)" is also used for a spiritual crisis in a journey towards union with God. Saint Thérèse of Lisieux, a 19th-century French Carmelite nun, wrote of her own experience. Centering on doubts about the afterlife, she reportedly told her fellow nuns, "If you only knew what darkness I am plunged into."

While this crisis is usually temporary in nature, it may last for extended periods. The "dark night" of Saint Paul of the Cross lasted 45 years. Mother Teresa of Calcutta, according to letters released in 2007, provided many instances of "dark nights," which lasted from 1948 almost up until her death in 1997, with only brief interludes of relief between. Franciscan Friar Father Benedict Groeschel, a friend of Mother Teresa for a large part of her life, claims that "the darkness left" towards the end of her life. Author Gary Zukov wrote an entire book called "The Dark Night of the Soul," and explains in depth these feelings of loss and despair. And these are only a few examples.

## My Own Dark Night

I plunged into a "dark night" at the age of 39. It was a period filled with terror, despair, and nothingness. I did not see the light at the end of the tunnel and was unable to feel even a glimmer of hope, happiness, or joy. The timing of going through a divorce and trying to take care of my young children was devastating. I attempted to pray and when I was able to leave the house, which was not often, I went to a chapel to talk to the Jesus statue there. I begged him for help.

# THE STORY

This intensely dark period has led to great light and awakening. My life is forever changed and I rarely even have a "bad" day anymore. I have so much access to higher conscious information now. This information guides me through every challenge and joy in my life. It truly is miraculous.

Jesus was a great example of miracle work and my understanding is that we too can experience miracles daily. He tells us what he did we shall do and more in John 14:12. I am always in awe of the miracles I regularly experience now and with great reverence, I expect them to occur. And so can you.

I wrote *Inner Visions—The Healing Path of Art* after I learned how to meditate and hear the incredible voice of intuition or God, my Higher Self, within me. I was then guided to share the divine messages in my artwork. I refer to this higher wisdom as "the Voice" throughout this book. This Voice is a spiritual team I work with and includes my Higher Self, God, many archangels, and ascended masters. I am clearly able to see, feel, hear, and know information from this Voice. It sounds like my own voice, but is powerfully knowing, wise, and accurate with its information to help me, my family, and so many people that I work with.

After I connected with the Voice, I was then guided to share the divine messages in my artwork. I was somewhat astonished at the synchronicity of finding a quote by Mohandas Gandhi about the Voice he heard:

> *For me, the voice of God, of Conscience, of Truth or the Inner Voice or 'the still small Voice' mean one and the same thing. I saw no form. I have never tried, for I have always believed God to be without form. One who realizes God is freed from sin for ever.... But what I did hear was like a Voice from afar and yet quite near. It was as unmistakable as some human*

> *voice definitely speaking to me, and irresistible. I was not dreaming at the time I heard the Voice. The hearing of the Voice was preceded by a terrific struggle within me. Suddenly the Voice came upon me. I listened, made certain that it was the Voice, and the struggle ceased. I was calm. The determination was made accordingly, the date and the hour of the fast were fixed.... Could I give any further evidence that it was truly the Voice that I heard and that it was not an echo of my own heated imagination? I have no further evidence to convince the skeptic. He is free to say that it was all self-delusion or hallucination. It may well have been so. I can offer no proof to the contrary. But I can say this—that not the unanimous verdict of the whole world against me could shake me from the belief that what I heard was the true voice of God.*

Where I left off in my first book became a whole new chapter in my life. As my story is now being written as a screenplay, I am guided to tell the miraculous story of how spiritual awakening cured my depression, inspired my purpose, and ignited the intuitive powers within. I am honored to share my story and then the original story of the journey through art.

## DOWNWARD SPIRAL

Feeling increasing fear and distress over having to end my marriage, not knowing my purpose and not feeling like I could take care of myself financially and support my children, my fearful thoughts began to consume me. I could not stand the thought of having to tell my children that they would have two households. I could not stand the pressure of a new job that had so much responsibility while my marriage was under such stress. I felt stuck and hopeless. How could I ever take care of

# THE STORY

myself, by myself and my children. How could I cause them such pain to split from their father?

Going to work each day with the new job was an unbearable pressure. When I quit, I came home, and things got worse. The realization that I had walked out on the one thing that was going to help me break free was unbearable. It sunk in that I had no job, a bad marriage, and if I had thought it was bad before, it got worse. Now I would never be able to leave. I had cut off my own financial freedom and had to face that I was now totally dependent on my husband, which made things worse. I felt hopeless and despondent.

I grew increasingly fearful that I would never work again and that I would never be independent and be able to care for myself and my children. A divorce was looming and I had no way to make it through. I thought about dying. I thought about my children. I went numb and paralyzed with fear. All feelings shut off. It was as though my mind was blank and numb and I could not feel any joy. The thoughts that I would die because I could not take care of myself and my children were constant.

I felt shattered. Hope was gone because I had walked out of a job that paid me well enough to get a divorce; now how the hell was I going to manage now without any work at all? How would I ever work again? I had gone through so many jobs and lost them all. Things were beyond bleak.

On top of that, everyone else seemed to know what they were doing. Why didn't I? Why did I not have a purpose? God was cruel. I had lost a job every year of my life. Why would God not help me take care of myself?? And my children? Why was everything so hard and impossible, such a struggle? If I couldn't work, I could not get a divorce. I would have to live with a man who was not right for me for the rest of my life, and I was not right for him. But I was stuck with no way out. Only misery is what I saw and felt.

Falling down around me was the fact that I had left the one way out—my job. Now what? I crashed for a month, fear of the future consuming me 24/7. I could not eat or sleep. I could only stare at the wall, chain smoke and attempt to take care of my children.

My husband cooked, cleaned, and functioned while I desperately tried to simply survive. Every fiber of my being felt dark and scared. The pain was excruciating on every level—emotionally, mentally, spiritually and physically. I was unable to function. I stared at the wall all day and night. I was literally paralyzed with fear. It was as though I could not feel at all, where nothing could pull me out of it.

Looking forward to anything was a foreign concept. The only thing I could feel was the constant pain of not feeling any hope, any joy or any peace. My whole being shut down. I was a shell. In that state, I remember praying. I did not know about meditation then, but had always loved Jesus and his teachings. I prayed and felt that there was no answer. I prayed anyway.

# A GLIMMER

After a month of not being able to function, praying constantly, and dragging myself to my favorite marble chapel, I sat in the chapel pew and talked to the large Jesus statue there. I had been going there for over a decade to talk to Jesus, Now I was imploring him to please answer my prayers.

Ten months later, I was able to go the local health food store, still just starting to function, where I picked up a free magazine called *Sacred Pathways*. I brought it home and saw an article called "Receiving The Divine" by Norman Paulsen, followed by an article on "Jesus the Yogi" by

# THE STORY

Yogananda, who brought Kriya Yoga to the West. I was fascinated with the article, which talked about heaven on earth, intuitive gifts and powers, meeting God face to face. I loved all of it.

I noticed in the bio that Yogananda had passed away, but Norman was alive and had lived in Yogananda's Self-Realization Fellowship in Los Angeles. I had a feeling then (that I now know was intuitive), that this man would change my life.

Somewhere, I read how a person with the Christ Consciousness could bestow it upon someone who wanted it. I thought, *I want that!!* I ordered the video tape and book called *Sacred Science Meditation, Transformation, Illumination*. I couldn't wait to get my materials.

Once they arrived, I read the book cover to cover and watched the tape. I learned about the Baptism of Fire and being anointed with the Holy Spirit. I did the Kriya Yoga meditation every day for weeks, sitting lotus style on my couch as the kids watched *Sponge Bob* on TV in the other room. I did not miss a day. I was determined to receive enlightenment and save myself.

One day, several weeks into my daily meditations, I was startled with a sudden realization. I called my husband into the room where I meditated. He came and sat down. I began to tell him that there was a "true spirit" we all had. It wasn't like our egos, and was always peaceful, always okay.

I couldn't get over my realization. With all the fear I had experienced, this new awareness was telling me everything was always okay?? Really?? It was mind blowing. He listened with interest while I continued to tell him about the magnitude of this realization.

That was a pivotal moment in my spiritual awakening. An inner voice was guiding me to understand that I was more than my ego. I felt a profound peace with this information, which meant that I was good. Not only that—everyone was!

I had felt badly about myself much of my life in many subtle ways. It was not anyone's fault; it was a consciousness that I was carrying. I became enlightened in that moment in which I realized that inherently, we have the nature of God. We have a true spirit.

I had been living my life based on a false self. This false self began to crumble with the awareness and connection now to who I truly was. We are all sparks of the Creator and have the ability to create our lives powerfully with this knowing. I know that the powerful Kriya Yoga meditation opened up and continues to open up deeper wisdom within me. I am able to clearly hear this guidance on a regular basis.

# SYNCHRONICITY

I had struggled for so long in terms of finding financial and emotional freedom. Knowing that my marriage was not going to work was a catalyst for me to try to get the help I knew I needed.

I bought a set of Tony Robbins tapes, called "Personal Power," and listened to the tapes every day. I remember clearly when his guest speaker, Barbara De Angelis, spoke about love. I had seen Barbara on TV, and knew her as the leading expert in the country on love. I heard her voice as I was in the kitchen doing the dishes, and I thought, *She sounds so professional, kind, and powerful I hope I can be a positive influence like her someday.*

I cried out to God in my kitchen that day. I felt like Scarlet O'Hara in *Gone With the Wind,* when after all she had been through, she proclaimed she would never go hungry again. I cried out to God, "God as my witness, may I never be financially and emotionally dependent again!" Back then, I depended on everyone except myself and in so many ways. The pain had become excruciating. Author Anais Nin describes this so clearly:

> *And the day came when the risk to remain tight in a bud was more painful than the risk it took to blossom.*

# HOPE

One weekend in December 2004, I was watching a Wayne Dyer marathon on PBS. During a break, I went into my kitchen, and noticed in my mind's eye, out of the blue, my painting Sunrise with words around it. I could see the actual book I wrote before I wrote it. I heard a voice say, "This is a book. You will write a book about your art and the meaning of the paintings."

I thought, *I could do that, like a coffee table book.* In that moment, I remembered college and my art history degree and realized I could write about my art as I had with all the papers about other artists. This time, it would be about me. WOW!

Instantly, I knew this was a big deal. I walked into my living room, grabbed some paper and a pen and wrote my first sentence. Then I wrote a paragraph. Something was alive and vibrant in me. I was connecting to a new sense of creativity and connection. I heard the new Voice. My life was forever changed!

# BETWEEN TWO WORLDS

It took one last bad night of fearful thoughts, too much alcohol, and my medication. I passed out late at night. I had been drinking too much yet fell asleep as I tried to meditate. All of a sudden, I was in space. It was pitch black, I was in the air, floating, and I could see stars around me in the blackness. My soul spoke, "I'm in space!"

Off to the right, I began to notice a white light. It was a white vortex of light, spiraling towards me. I could hear a sound that I can only describe as the sound of creation. It was a loud and deep OM, very loud and deep. I thought, *This is what Norman talked about in his book! The baptism of fire! The Christ light is coming towards me. It's going to go through me!!*

The vortex of light came closer and I was getting more elated. *It's happening!* I closed my eyes and the light went through me, vibrating. I was not scared. It was changing my DNA and my energy field. The baptism of fire I experienced can be described as follows (from Norman Paulsen's book, *Sacred Science*):

> *The Baptism of Fire is the projected light and energy emanating directly from Christ Consciousness within and around the body of Christ, the hub from which the expanding spheres of creation now spin. I AM THAT I AM, Mother and Father, descending in vortexes of white fire, bring about the conception and birth of the divine Christ child within the bridal chamber of the heart. As I AM THAT I AM descends within the duel sacred forces of Christ, the physical body is wrapped within a cocoon of brilliant white light, like white fire, by feminine force, as the masculine force enters at the crown of the head.*

My Higher Self and the Christ Light took over the bad job my lower self was doing, running my life into the ground.

That was February 3, 2005. I later found out, February 3rd is Norman Paulsen's birthday. It was surely a rebirth for me. It was a dawning of a new consciousness for me. Life was soon to get really good.

## THE STORY

# A Dream Forms

For decades, doctors had told me that I would always need to take medication to combat my depression and anxiety. It wasn't long after the beginning of writing my book that I went off of medication, never to return. When I first started writing, I felt as though I was the only one without a dream.

We are supposed to follow our dreams, but what if we didn't have any dreams to begin with? I was more than familiar with the feeling of "supposed to being doing something," but was never quite sure what. Now I was writing a book. This was more than just "something"—this was a miracle.

I had never gotten good grades in writing or English. Other people wrote, not me. I never felt like I had anything to say. What I felt now was different, though. Words were coming through me. I didn't have to think about what to write. It was like the book was writing itself. I could not believe it was so easy. Writing the whole book took less than a month.

The next step was publishing my book. I didn't know anything about that either. A few trips to my "second home," Barnes and Noble, and voilá, I found books on agents and publishing. I devoted my time to learning everything I could about publishing. I was not going to write a book and not publish it, that I knew. I wrote many proposals and query letters and got back respectful replies about how stunning my artwork was, but they did not feel my religious point of view agreed with theirs. Well, I was a spiritual writer and was not deterred.

It dawned on me to look up Norman Paulsen, since I had mentioned his name and Kriya Yoga in my book. I thought it would be nice to let him know that. I learned that he had founded Sunburst Sanctuary in

Lompoc, California, located his number, called him, and he answered the phone in person.

While my two boys played with their toy cars in the next room, I very clearly heard Norman's strong God-like voice on the other end of the line. I told him about my book and that he was mentioned in it. He asked how the publishing process was going. I said it wasn't going so well, and he replied that it wasn't easy to get a spiritual book published. He then told me that he had had the same problem with his book *Christ Consciousness and Sacred Science,* so he had published it himself. Maybe he would publish my book. He told me he would consult with Spirit and call me back. I almost fell over.

Norman called back the very next day and told me he would like to publish my book for free. Then he invited me to come to Sunburst Sanctuary in California, with all expenses paid. This was the next biggest miracle I had experienced since meditating. Of course, I said yes, and did my best to express my profound gratitude.

I told my husband and my children. Since my husband had read the manuscript and told me it was really good, he had an idea that I was about to embark on something big. My kids, always loving, were fine. Some friends thought it was crazy. "People don't do that, publish your book, fly you for free there." I replied that Christ Conscious people do.

I had trusted my intuition, even though I didn't really know what that was yet, nor had I really realized how intuitive I was becoming.

# THE STORY

## MEETING NORMAN

No one was happier than I was to take an early flight out of Boston to California in June of 2005. I was incredulous the whole way there, telling people in the airport restaurants that my book was being published, as if I had won the lottery. I almost missed my flight from Los Angeles to Santa Barbara because I was so engrossed in socializing on my way there. On the last leg of the trip, from LA to Santa Barbara, some friends left messages warning me to be careful and wondering if I really knew what I was doing. I had never been more sure.

I was greeted at the airport by one of the Sanctuary members, who drove me back to the retreat center. Norman had provided me with my own log cabin, all to myself. Rosemary and other herbs grew wild just outside my door. My "chauffeur" suggested I take a nap and told me I was to meet Norman at 6:30 pm.

I could not believe I was about to meet my spiritual mentor. His words in book and tape meant that I was no longer gripped by darkness and sadness. I ran to the meeting hall to meet him. After a big hug, he asked me to sit facing him. Along with the experience in space, meeting Norman face to face was a highly spiritual experience in which he bestowed me with more of the Christ Consciousness, as he had described in that first article.

Norman looked at me for a moment, called on Spirit and delivered a message to me. He took his hand in an upward motion as if to the sky, then drew a line down as if to the earth. He said, "You have come from Heaven to help the earth."

*Wow*, I thought, *that might be true, but I've never heard anyone say that about ME.* I nodded my head yes. This was all so miraculous. Something supernatural was happening. I told him about the meditation experience I had in space and he affirmed that I had received the Baptism of Fire, the anointing of the Holy Spirit.

What an amazing meeting! I spent the weekend at the Sanctuary, meditating with Norman and the community at 6 a.m. and after dinner. After Sunday service, he introduced me to his editor and told me she would be editing my book and that they would then publish it.

A profound peace welled up within me. I felt so much gratitude that I still have trouble putting it into words. I had told the friends who had not believed in my trip that this trip would forever change my life and help my children. My intuition, as always, was spot on.

I had yet to realize that my intuitive gifts and dormant healing powers were preparing to be unleashed. My experience with Norman could help me serve countless people in ways still to be revealed.

## Back to Reality

When I returned home from California, I found it much easier to find work in the corporate world. Even though I had lost or left two jobs while writing and publishing my book, it didn't really matter. I had discovered a purpose within that kept me buoyant despite these challenges.

One employer actually let me go once he discovered I had a website and my book was about to be published. He said I should be doing something more creative. With my pending divorce and not yet being a bestselling author, I still needed a job to be independent and take care of my children. I bawled my eyes out while putting my desk knick-knacks in a box, walking the walk of shame to my car. I had just been fired. Back to square one.

# THE STORY

During this time, Norman's editor was working on my book, which helped keep hope alive for me.

I found another job and the day the book was delivered to my door, I was fired that day from that job. They told me it was a business decision. Was talking about my new book a threat to my employers? I have no doubt that it was. In addition, I was getting the "cosmic boot." Apparently, the Universe had other plans for me. It sure did!

I drove home fired and got on the computer. My editor had a suggestion that I attend Mark Victor Hansen's Mega Book Marketing event in Florida. *Well, I don't have a job. I'll go!* That intuitive Voice was speaking very loudly. I spoke back to it: *I don't have the money.* I heard, *Go anyway.* Putting the trip on a credit card, I packed my bags.

## A NEW REALITY BEGINS

Life was feeling more exciting, that was for sure. I was hopping on another plane, now as an author on a mission. I missed my kids terribly, calling them often, and at the same time, I had a deep knowing that by following my dream and intuition, I would be teaching my boys priceless lessons: follow your heart and know that your dreams matter.

I sat with 500 other authors for three days listening to Mark and his amazing group of speakers. When Mark said, "Your book is an empire," I could hardly believe it. My heart leapt for joy. A book is not just a book, it's an empire! Part of me thought, *How in the world is that possible?* For a chronic job loser like myself, an empire certainly sounded promising. Maybe I really could create a solid new life.

When Barbara De Angelis took the stage on the morning of the last day, it was electrifying. She has the kind of power as a speaker that will transform you. When she offered the opportunity to work with her, I couldn't run to the back of the room to sign up with her quickly enough. My inner Voice was speaking loudly and clearly.

What I didn't know then was that I was about to transform EVERYTHING in my life for good.

Back home again, I found another job to make ends meet. My divorce was underway and now, I was working with Barbara De Angelis, a wonderful bestselling author. She is a love expert who spiritually transforms lives with her work.

While my divorce was final, we could not yet afford to live apart. We stayed in the same home for an entire year after the divorce as I worked with Barbara and prepared myself for a new life.

## BUILDING AN EMPIRE

As I worked with Barbara and learned how to do intuitive readings, I also began an online business. My first website was born from a connection with the webmaster for a company for which I was working. He was creating the company website and I worked the front desk. One day, he was waiting to speak to the owner and we began to talk. I had just finished my manuscript and told him I was an artist and an author. He asked if I had a website. I did not.

He began to tell me that if I had a website, even people from Japan could see my artwork. I was floored. I got his contact info and later he created my first website, Inner Visions Gallery. I sold my art and book on this site. It was amazing.

I was then mentored on how to create a successful business online. I used my ex-husband's computer, for at the time, did not own one myself.

I spent hours every day after work and at night when the kids went to sleep, building my business. That business now supports an income for myself and my family.

I am one of the growing number of heart-centered entrepreneurs. This business continues to help me make a great income from my products and services, and allows me to assist people all over the world. My latest international clients have been from France and India. After I showed my boss my website, he fired me. I think he did me a favor. I am now on my fourth website, www.yourintuitivemakeover.com.

## WORKING WITH BARBARA DE ANGELIS

With faith, I went to Barbara's Breakthrough Workshop in Palm Springs, California, in the spring of 2007. It was a weekend workshop that I knew I had to attend. Once there, I sat down feeling like a stranger in a strange land, yet very excited to work with Barbara and gain the strength I needed to move forward.

Immediately, I noticed a good-looking man in the seat in front of me to the right. I thought, *He looks like trouble.* When Barbara told us to get into groups, despite my trepidation, I boldly walked up to him and asked him to be in my group. His name was Dean. He later told me I looked haunted and sad.

Later that weekend, Dean was in my group again. When our group shared the best thing in our lives, he said basketball, and I said being a good mom to my kids. Softly, he said, "That's great." Intuitively, I heard *You are going to marry him.*

I signed up to continue working with Barbara for another year. Dean had as well. A year of miracles and transformation was underway when I flew to retreats in Angel Valley, Sedona, and Palm Springs several times that year to meet with our Transformation Circle, led by our Guru Barbara.

I quit smoking and focused on healing myself. Dean and I were nothing more than friends, working through lifetimes of pain to find forgiveness and light after the dark times we had experienced. He, too, was trying to work through a divorce. Every weekend retreat with Barbara and the group was filled with tears and pain transforming into light. She led us through exercises we did together and as a group, sharing spiritual wisdom and helping all of us heal our pain. Barbara talked openly about the Great Beings with us helping us do this work. I felt like I had come home.

During her "Successful Speaking" course, Barbara suggested that I take a speaking risk, so I signed up for my first live event, an Intuitive Arts Expo in Rhode Island. I had purchased some Goddess oracle cards and purchased a vendor table with a friend to try my first-ever intuitive readings. My friend shot me a look when someone sat at my table for a 15-minute reading for $25, as if to say "Good Luck" wink wink, because I'd need it.

I drew some cards for my "client" and lo and behold, I starting talking to the woman about clearing a space in her home to do work. She told me she had spent her whole weekend doing that. *Of course you have*, I thought. *I can't believe I was right!!*

I kept going and told the woman what I saw. For the rest of the day, I had a line of people waiting for my readings.

A woman at a nearby table saw how popular my readings were and introduced herself to me as the editor of a magazine. She knew someone who could certify me as an angel reader. A what? I had never heard of

# THE STORY

that. I went home, looked up the person who could certify me, and signed up for her course.

The Voice was very clear. *This will help you financially and will help you help others the way you have wanted.*

Now, along with my book, I was now a Certified Angel Reader, connecting to the angelic realm. Not many people knew what I was talking about when I told them this, but gradually, I started to connect with people who did. I also did readings for all my Transformation friends, of course with Barbara's permission.

My new life wasn't so weird after all. Later on that editor published my articles in her magazine, *Aspire*. I was now a published, self-help article writer as well.

## MOVING OUT AND MOVING ON

Throughout our work together, Barbara told me I could not help other people live their dreams, like I felt I should be doing, unless I had my ex-husband move out. I could not help other people until I helped myself. I could not have been more scared to really have him go. There was so much at stake: our home of 12 years, our children… What if we couldn't make it financially? Surviving my dark night of the soul, writing my book, receiving the white light initiation, meeting Norman, and now working with Barbara and doing readings, certainly helped me realize that I was not alone and that maybe I could be OK.

The day after Thanksgiving in 2007, my ex-husband moved out. I felt like a 2-by-4 had hit me. I had some savings but not much. I had quit my last job, and was now living off my meager savings and credit cards to be able to travel to Barbara's retreats.

# MIRACULOUS

I felt that I wouldn't last long without a job. I applied and was hired by a chain restaurant. Some days, I made $30 at lunch and other times $80. Now completely on my own, this up-and-down was somewhat terrifying. It seemed like it snowed every other day as well.

My ex had taken a lot of the furniture and I was sleeping on a mattress on the floor of an empty bedroom. When my boys were at their father's and I was alone, I cried often. I hit bottom one morning when I realized I would not be able to pay my mortgage payment, or in fact, any of my bills. I knew that the threat of losing my home was real. I could not afford to turn the heat on in January, and wore layers of sweaters and coats indoors. I questioned my decision to have my ex move out.

After tearfully praying to God one morning, I said, "Thank You. Thank You, God, that I am alive. If this is all I have, I thank you." I meant it. I felt relief. I had surrendered.

I flew to Arizona for Barbara's last retreat in April of 2008. Photos taken of me during the retreat were the best I have ever taken. My new strength and lightness are visible. I look happy, content, and at peace. I had nothing in terms of material living, but I sure had my spiritual self. That was priceless.

I knew my year with Barbara was ending. At the final ceremony, Barbara graced us all with gifts and blessings from the Divine. She told me in front of our group that I was meant to be one of the most powerful healers on the planet as directed by the Higher Beings working with her. She blessed me with abundance and my soul mate. I remember Dean being blessed with the same.

I flew home to my empty house. The kids were at their father's place for the weekend. I got a call from Dean. We talked and talked on the phone. He was in California, I was in New Hampshire. We talked every day for a week. He then told me he was in love with me. Right after that, I received a call from my brother regarding the family business. I was to receive a windfall buyout that was beyond my comprehension. I was now set financially and love was knocking at my door!

The miracles brought into my life from my spiritual awakening astonish, surprise, and delight me daily. Dean moved across the country and we got married. I have built a life that aligns with my being and now help others do the same. Those early angel readings have evolved into a flourishing intuitive coaching business. Today, I have the honor of working with people all over the world, helping them heal their wounds, find their gifts and talents, and encourage them to find and live their dreams.

# Intuitive Healing and Coaching and The Voice

Intuitively, I knew when I created my first website that I wanted to add "Intuitive Coaching." I was confident in doing intuitive readings, but had never coached. Nonetheless, I added this service based on an intuitive feeling and knowing. Years went by without a single coaching client until one day, a large sum of money appeared in my PayPal account.

Someone had ordered a one-hour reading and a four-week coaching program at the same time. I could have panicked because I did not have a coaching program, but I didn't. I told the Voice that I needed a coaching program. That weekend, I was completely guided on what to do. I would clear, heal, and activate the seven spiritual centers in the body known as chakras. I just did it rather than letting doubt or panic slip in.

# MIRACULOUS

The information from the first day with that client until now guides me with information about their wounds as well as their gifts, talents, strengths, and abilities. I work with their guides and angels and mine along with Spirit. A spiritual team comes through me to help facilitate healing, enhance inner power, and more with each client. It is like clearing out the weeds to see the garden. I do this with people on the phone from all over the country. I have coached every week of the year since that first client. It is intuitive energy work and it is miraculous.

When I work with clients, once we release their false beliefs, I often receive and share the titles of books they are meant to write or the names of workshops and coaching programs they are meant to facilitate. I have received information on new businesses for people and many are now online, creating a new source of income while serving others.

I speak and present to hundreds of people, and thousands have listened to my radio and television shows. I have created a deck of oracle cards from my artwork and divine channeling that facilitates higher consciousness.

The psychic intuitive floodgates have opened for me as I channel information from my Higher Self and our divine guides to help clients release pain and live more fully in peace and happiness. A divine energy flows through me as I facilitate this healing energy as I work with clients. My miracles become their miracles. They have started businesses, healed their relationships, started living their life purpose, written books, gotten published, are doing healing work, and help others as well. I have written two more books and am sure there are more on the way.

# The *Extreme Intuitive Makeover* Story

Two years ago, the Voice told me the name of my last book, *Extreme Intuitive Makeover*. I had a pen and paper and wrote it all down. I was to write this book, create a CD set to go along with it, and transform people in mind, body, and spirit. I had seen popular makeover shows about houses, haircuts, physical transformations with diet and wardrobe. My Voice was guiding me to transform people's lives. For years, I felt this book coming into reality. Last January, in 20 hours, it came through. I have been blessed with the wonderful publishing services from Kira and HenschelHaus Publishing. The book has received profound testimonials and is a basis for many workshops and programs I offer today. In 2013, the book became a bestseller!

# Client Stories

The Universe is amazing and supportive of our journeys. As I have learned to allow the Law of Attraction, or what I call "The Law of Alignment," to work in my life, miracles continue to occur. Recently, a woman from France emailed me. She was visiting the United States and happened into a Barnes and Noble bookstore. My book, *Extreme Intuitive Makeover 55 Keys to Health, Wealth, and Happiness,* leapt off the shelf into her hands. She read it cover to cover and knew that this was the answer to her prayers. She contacted me and I worked with her in my Virtual One-Day Retreat, 9 am-3 pm via Skype, certifying her as a Professional Intuitive. She had a natural gift and I was happy to clear any blocks in the way and certify her to make a living and serve others in France and worldwide with her intuitive gifts.

I worked with Amy, a fifty-ish woman from Massachusetts, who attended my first "Evening of Divine Messages Workshop" in 2008. Participants said it was "not a workshop, but a spiritual experience." I taught them Kriya Yoga Meditation and helped them learn to connect with the Angelic Realm. Amy was so moved from the workshop that she contacted me afterwards, telling me that she knew I could help her. At the time, I was doing phone readings, but Amy wanted to see me in person. She drove two hours to come to my home, where I worked with her for an hour.

Many people had told Amy that she should write. She came to me not knowing how to do so and feeling awful about it. I called on her highest guides and angels and mine, as well as Divine Spirit. I then shifted her energy to allow writing to come through. She now has a radio show and publishes an article weekly answering people's questions as she connects to the angelic realm. You can find her here: www.askangelamy.com

After every presentation I give, people now come up to me just as I did with my mentor, Barbara De Angelis and I coach them in my programs. I also have an Inner Circle of very loyal clients who take my classes and personally coach with me. We dialog daily on Facebook. This is a core group of women who are wonderfully gifted; I am honored to help them discover their gifts more fully. They share these gifts with others. I think they will change the world. Here are some Inner Circle stories.

Mary, in her fifties, from New York, joined my Inner Circle in 2010. She also took my Angel Reader Certification Course, meeting on the

# THE STORY

phone for an hour for six weeks. Upon completion of the course, she is now giving angel messages to people all over the world, as well as leading group angel classes in her home. She is delighted to use her gift and help so many. Through learning to open to her intuition and with my guidance, she now also does mediumship readings, in which she connects with loved ones who have passed on. Mary helps heal, comfort, and soothe souls everywhere. You can find out more about Mary's readings at www.fromheavenabovereadingbymary.com/index.html

Anna Marie, in her sixties, from Massachusetts, joined my Inner Circle after she discovered my work from another spiritual teacher. A colleague of mine took my oracle cards to her workshop and had people pull cards. Anna selected a card and received a message that meant so much to her, she contacted me for coaching. I have been working with her for almost two years now and we meet on the phone every month. She is working on her poetry book, writing *Divine Poems from Spirit,* and I will help her publish it. She also paints beautiful intuitive paintings and will illustrate her poetry book with her artwork. She helps others with healing and intuitive readings. Anna Marie recently took my class on writing. She is now an expert author on e-zine articles. She has overcome depression and breast cancer and shares her wisdom here: amnickie.wordpress.com/

Amber, in her forties, from Georgia, joined my Inner Circle and coaching program. She also enjoys every class I teach. She has overcome doubt and insecurity and gained confidence in herself that has allowed her great emotional freedom. She is now writing and channeling the Higher Realms and we are putting together a workshop for her to help and empower battered women as she helps them find their inner strength and beauty. She is also a Certified Angel Reader, graduating from my course, and is now helping others in a beautiful way receive messages of love, comfort, and inspiration.

Katie, in her thirties, from Ohio and a member of my Inner Circle, also coached with me on my TV show and in personal coaching classes. She was unhappy with her job, a single mother in a dismal relationship. Through our coaching, she has found her calling as a physician's assistant and energy healer. Her relationship has improved, most importantly, with herself.

Leanna, in her thirties, from Massachusetts, saw me speak and signed up to work with me. She was stuck in a bad relationship, afraid to move forward in her life, and had no passion or purpose. Through working with me, she now understands her purpose, is becoming a certified yoga instructor, and although her boyfriend broke up with her, she is thriving. Our latest coaching session revealed to her a coaching program that will help so many.

A wife and mother, Amanda, in her thirties, from California, in my Inner Circle, began coaching with me. She asked me for more coaching after the program was over, so I created a longer program for her. She takes my classes and is now a powerful healer, working on opening her own healing center, and no longer feels bored in her life. Her beautiful photographs can be seen here: www.reflectionsbyamandamartin.com

Cheryl, in her fifties, from Massachusetts, is in my Inner Circle. She has had the same job for over 25 years, and knew there was something more. Five years ago, she sent me a check out of the blue to paint her an inspirational painting. Her faith in my work from the beginning means so much. She had seen my article in *Aspire* magazine. I gave her many readings before I had a coaching program, then she coached with me, as well as taking my classes. She does powerful readings as she connects to the angelic realm, now has a beautiful website, and enjoys empowering

## THE STORY

people through her writing, coaching and workshops. Cheryl's beautiful website is here: www.depthandwisdom.net/

Val, in her fifties, is from Maine and part of my Inner Circle. She is an animal communicator and healer. She took my writing class and is now an expert author on e-zine articles. Her blog is thriving and she is now a published self-help writer. Her mission is to help bring love, light, and laughter to pets and the people that share their lives. Visit her website at www.thepawsitivepath.com/

Saskia, in her thirties, from Massachusetts, attended my presentation at a recent Natural Living Expo. I was happy to connect with her after my talk. She has been coaching with me and I was thrilled when the name of her coaching program came through me intuitively. I knew that she had a gift as a healer and since the title "9 Steps to Emotional Freedom" came through for her, she has been writing a book, creating retreats, and recording CDs to go with this information. Saskia's powerful healing work can be found here: www.fallinginlovewithlife.com

I also teach live and virtual all-day workshops, Here are some testimonials from my most recent one:

*I am soooo looking forward to your next teleclass. I thoroughly enjoyed your previous offering, more than I ever expected! It was "leaps and bounds" beyond others I've participated in with different facilitators.* —Anna N., Massachusetts

*I don't know why I went to the information session, nor why I signed up for the workshop! But I did, and am so glad that I did. Anne does not skimp with her time nor her attention!*

*The insights that Anne channeled were nothing short of astounding, and the entire experience uplifting and heart opening. As strange as it sounds to me as I write it, I have found a new lightness in my being. Forgiveness – the place to begin to resolve so many of our self-induced limitations. I would recommend Anne to anyone wanting to clear their chakras and find new openness, understanding and peace.*
—Evelyn, Nashua, NH

*I was very surprised that the chakra clearing workshop shed light on some old and buried wounds for me, allowing for more effective healing. It also brought out some very fundamental truths, which in turn both provided for more clarity of purpose, and inspiration to pursue that purpose. Just what I needed! Thank you, Anne!*
—Amber F, NH

## INNER VISIONS

"Dreams—*we are told to follow them*...." This opening line from Anne Deidre's book is so true, but rare is the person who does follow them. This book is the journey of Anne following her dreams through a difficult time in her life and how by following her dream of painting, it helped to bring her out of depression and into the light. Often we think we cannot do something, like painting, because we have not studied it or received training, but Anne just did it and found she could "capture her feelings." This brought her joy, insight and helped lead her to a spiritual path. That in turn led her to develop her intuition, to desire to learn how to meditate and to the ability to find peace during difficult times.

## THE STORY

What inspired me was the thought that I could do that too, just for me, not for anyone else and what hidden insights and surprises might I find. This is a simple story that is everyone's story, to encourage us to follow our dreams. —Nancy Belton, Sunburst Sanctuary

# FACING THE NUMBER-ONE FEAR IN LIFE

There is a level of profound appreciation and gratitude that I now carry as I do book signings and speaking engagements.

It was during Mark Victor Hansen's Mega Book Marketing Event in the summer of 2006 where he told us a book was a business. Not only that, but a book does not sell itself, we must speak about it. With my bouts of anxiety and agoraphobia, avoiding crowds and people, I was a little nervous upon hearing this news.

I had developed an intense fear of public speaking starting in my twenties. Nonetheless, at my first chance, I offered to do a free seminar at the New Age Expo in Peabody, MA in the summer of 2007. Fifty people watched as my hands and voice shook while I stumbled over my notes. I thought I had written enough material to cover the hour I was to speak, and had even bought a watch with a big face on it, so proud was I to be facing my fear.

After just 10 minutes, I looked at the big watch on my wrist and panicked. I had fifty minutes to fill the time but had nothing left to read from my notes!!! I thought about running out of the room to grab my angel cards. *No,* I told myself, *I can't leave everyone sitting here!* I prayed while I kept talking and looked at the audience.

Suddenly my intuitive Voice spoke, instructing me to talk about the chakras, the seven primary spiritual centers in our physical bodies that are connected to Spirit. I took a deep breath and began to channel information to the audience about the chakras. The time flew by and I noticed the time keeper at the back of the room holding up a sign, "10 minutes left." I couldn't believe it! People came up to me afterwards to tell me I had inspired them and changed their lives. I learned a valuable lesson in trust that day, allowing and believing in that inner voice to guide me.

I spoke a few more times and it had gotten easier but was yet to be something that I really enjoyed. I had a speaking breakthrough in the fall of 2011. I had a booth at the two-day event sponsored by *Spirit of Change* magazine, the Natural Living Expo. Many thousands of people came by my table and I was busy both days all day doing readings, selling books and my oracle cards. My presentation of *Your Intuitive Life Makeover* was slotted for 3 pm Sunday, the last day of the event. Maybe three people had come up to me, saying they would attend. It was 2:45 pm and I was finishing up a reading when I realized the time. I completed the reading, gathered my materials and ran to the seminar room thinking, maybe no one would show up. I was actually hoping this as I ran to the room.

When I turned the corner and looked in the door, I saw that every seat was filled and there was standing room only. Not only that, the event manager was starting to turn people away. The room was packed. I gulped with humility. As I slowly walked to the front of the room, many thoughts and emotions filled my mind. My heart had taken over. I experienced deep humility and gratitude all at once as I profoundly realized the honor and privilege it was to have so many people waiting to listen to me speak.

Since then, I have never been afraid to speak. When the CD seminar company put a microphone on me to record my presentation, I looked out at the sea of over a 100 faces and I felt love for each and every one. I

# THE STORY

vowed to myself to always remember this moment and always thank God for my ability to serve. I warmly greeted my audience and then began to share my story and then channel messages from the divine realms.

I speak regularly now, going back to this event each year, and warmly greet my audience and enjoy every moment I spend with them.

I am thankful to receive the praise and feedback of the many people who hear me speak, telling me that I inspired them and gave them hope. I am happy that I work with many of them in my long-term elite coaching program. I love helping them find their voices, too.

## AT BOOKSTORES NATIONWIDE

Finding that my book was now on the Barnes and Noble bookshelves across the country was a surreal moment. The understanding of the impact I am able to make through my work continues to amaze me. I had a book signing at my local Barnes and Noble bookstore last fall. Dean and I enjoyed the celebrity feeling as he told me he felt like one too just being next to me. As we walked into the front entrance, we saw a larger than life poster of me and my book. Humility washed over again with gratitude as I walked to my author's table piled with my books.

Another life-size poster of me stood on the table. A little girl of about 8 and her dad stopped to see what was going on. The little girl's jaw dropped as she looked at the poster, then me, back at the poster, then me. She exclaimed "Is that YOU?" I smiled, greeted her, and said yes. Her dad told me she loves to read. I asked the little girl her name, shook her hand, and told her to keep on reading. I realized that she felt like she had seen a famous person.

# MIRACULOUS

I do enjoy meeting so many people, touching so many lives and feeling the fulfillment of my dreams coming true while serving others. As I continue to do radio and TV interviews, speak to large groups, and coach so many people, I am deeply grateful for everything I have done. I have shown my children that dreams can come true and that they can honor their gifts and talents, express their creativity, and enjoy their lives.

My older son, Jake, is now a highly prolific songwriter. He writes easily, rhyming his words while creatively expressing deep emotional depth. He is a confident and loving young man.

My younger son, Brandon, gets straight As and is a star Lacrosse player. He had some struggles at an early age where teachers wanted to medicate him, for he was very active. I met with them, refused to give the recommended medications, and changed schools to help him get the support he needed. At his new school, he had a wonderful teacher who not only liked him but saw his brilliance. No medication, just As. His teachers love him and often comment on his above average-abilities and graciousness and kindness. My intuitive voice knew my child. All is perfect.

What a great time to be alive. If you have suffered the way I have, know that you are here for a purpose. Your spiritual connection can heal all your wounds and carry you to great heights. I'll see you there.

# The Messages

What follows is the original book of *Inner Visions: The Healing Path of Art*. I had a dream a few months ago, in which this book landed in my hands. I heard a voice thanking me for writing it, for sitting down and bringing it into reality, and for sharing the messages of faith, hope, and love. What I have learned and what I know is that I do not work alone. My Higher Self, Jesus, Buddha, Archangel Michael, Archangel Gabriel, and some other Masters of Light, along with God, help me with this work. I pray that my work blesses you.

# INNER VISIONS
## THE HEALING PATH OF ART

This section of the book was originally published in 2006 by Sunburst Publishing under ISBN 978-0-941848-17-6.

It was dedicated to the creative artist within each person —that spark of the Divine that gives us life.

# FOREWORD

This profound little book of pure innocence has captured in visual art form the human emotions within the awakening soul! Anne Smith's sensitive form of expression touches on a common cord of our universal connectedness as she courageously unveils her true nature in *Inner Visions*.

She shares her own life story and the universal challenges to which we can all relate. She turns the human emotional hardships into positive affirmations, as she offers a sense of hope in her words and visual art. She touches on a human cord that opens up our heart and soul to experience who we really are, to touch and reconnect to our true nature, the divine imprint of God's love within our souls.

Anne's visual images and inspirations of encouragement convey a sense of hope in the process of finding ourselves it the midst of the doubts, fears, and judgments we place on ourselves. She conveys throughout her writings and visual art her strong sense of faith in God's infinite mercy. It is her strong faith that inspires her to go beyond dogma and touch the universal truth that is the pure essence of all religions— unconditional love and forgiveness for ourselves and others.

It is through this process that we will begin to uncover the ocean of God's creative expression of love within our souls. We need only to trust in ourselves as we make the effort to tap into this wondrous reserve. Anne Smith is someone who has made that effort, and may her works inspire others to find the key to unlock the flow of their own creativity and souls wisdom through the instrument of this book.

— Norman Paulsen

# Introduction

This is the story of the beginning of my journey towards transcendence. I first saw articles in *Sacred Pathways* magazine in December of 2004, by Paramahansa Yogananda, "Jesus the Yogi: Resurrection of the Christ Within You." and his direct disciple, Norman Paulsen's "Christ Consciousness: Receiving the Divine." At the time, I was struggling to believe that rising above my problems was possible, and had yet to realize—actually experience—the reality of this transcendence.

The articles described the possibility of receiving the Divine, awakening the Divine within ourselves, and I knew instantly that this was what I had been searching for. I contacted the Solar Logos Church that Norman founded and ordered his book and tape on how to practice the meditation he spoke of in the article. After practicing this technique, soon I was writing, painting again, and creating. Tapping into my soul's purpose became possible for me when I began practicing Kriya Yoga meditation.

I was blessed to visit Norman Paulsen at Sunburst Sanctuary in June 2005. It was so meaningful to sit down with him in person and describe to him the meditation experiences I had in the past few months. In his article, "Christ Consciousness: Receiving the Divine," Norman had described the Baptism of Fire. When I read about that, I remember thinking, *How incredible!*

On February 3, 2005, I had gone to sleep in a meditative state. Suddenly, I awakened in this state and realized I was in space. My soul spoke aloud as I beheld a dark sky filled with stars. Soon I noticed a light ahead on the right of my view. It was spiraling, and I knew from the article in Sacred Pathways that this was the Baptism of Fire. Norman describes it like this:

> *The Baptism of Fire is the projected light and energy emanating directly from Christ Consciousness within and around the body of Christ, the hub from which the expanding spheres of creation now spin. I AM THAT I AM, Mother and Father, descending in vortexes of white fire, bring about the conception and birth of the divine Christ child within the bridal chamber of the heart. As I AM THAT I AM descends within the dual sacred forces of Christ, the physical body is wrapped within a cocoon of brilliant white light, like white fire, by the feminine force, as the masculine force enters at the crown of the head.*

I saw this light and heard the sound that is difficult to describe: the powerful sound of the energy of the universe. I thought, "It's coming toward me; this is good." I closed my eyes as it came toward me and soon, I felt it envelop and go through me at once in a louder, vibrationally lifting sensation. I thought, "Finally!" and felt thorough joy and bliss.

I awoke and looked at the clock. It was 3:07 a.m.. I realized the enormity of what had just happened and felt a sense of deep peace. Since that experience—the dawning of Christ Consciousness within me—my life has continued to improve. It's not that challenges don't continue to arise, but I have found that along with the challenges, it makes all the difference to realize who I am as a daughter of God, and what is now possible. It is a core sense of strength. This consciousness helps me feel joy within any sorrow and to understand the joy inherent in giving from the heart.

Being at Sunburst Sanctuary was uplifting and moving on so many levels. Meeting Norman was an honor. He and his wife Patty welcomed me into their family at the sanctuary. Nancy Belton, an integral part of the sanctuary, was wonderful to me. I know that we are all connected with Spirit and the positive energy there was remarkable. As well as the personal opportunity to spiritually retreat, I was able to participate in the daily meditations.

Meditating at 6 a.m. with Norman, Patty, Nancy, and others in the community made me grateful in knowing they are doing planetary good for so many. After the Sunday service, Norman and Nancy made it possible for me to meet with Dawn King, who has typeset, edited, and turned this material into a book with her loving expertise.

I used to think I could do it on my own. Although I have always prayed, a part of me was holding back. Since these experiences, I know that when I let God in, His will for me is so much more than what I was trying to do on my own. Thank you, Norman Paulsen, for helping me make my publishing dream a reality and for showing me a path to higher consciousness and awakening my Pure Self.

I wish blessings, peace, and joy to all on their spiritual journeys.

—Anne Smith

# Inner Visions

Dreams—we're told to follow them, but what if we don't know where to begin, and we feel like we don't have any to begin with? That's where I found myself a year ago. Hitting bottom as the saying goes, had become a constant state. Walking out on a job was something I had never done before. Dealing with the emotions that led up to this decision and the excruciating pain of walking away from the wonderful opportunity that had presented itself, was something I was not prepared for.

I had been a successful assistant property manager/leasing consultant for two years. At the start it was a job with which I had no previous experience, but one in which I quickly found myself enjoying a feeling of being in control, and gaining confidence in my abilities. It was a nurturing environment. Through the people I worked with and the residents at the different properties we managed, I was able to turn my weaknesses into strengths and grow towards my potential. I looked forward to work each day. After work and on the weekends I was able to let work go, and found comfort in that.

We had plenty of time to plan for the end that was coming. The owners, who had always been wonderful to me, told us that they were selling the property where our office was located. I think that we were in denial for many months. Eventually I realized that I had to seek new employment—they could not tell me how much longer I would have a job.

Because of my incredible experience with this company, those I worked with and the residents I had come to know as friends, I felt self-assured scanning the job classified ads to find out what new opportunities were out there. This was October of 2003. I responded to an ad for property manager. Perhaps it was a little beyond my experience, but I had faith that I could do the job. After one interview I was hired. Gratitude filled my heart, and I was looking forward to the challenges ahead of me. Yet, I was sad to leave a job where I had been so happy.

My new coworkers and the owner of the company could not have been more welcoming. I, however, began to experience doubt in my abilities. Within a month this doubt had grown to an overwhelming state of anxiety. This state of mind paralyzed me. Now I was unable to sleep, which meant no reprieve from the pain and fear that gripped me. I held on for ten weeks. I was honest with them about my fears and they responded with such kindness and confidence in me that it was doubly heartbreaking when I realized that I could not hang in there.

I left this job without having another one to go to. It was February—bitter cold. Depressing hardly covers the devastation I felt. I had kept in contact with former employers from a past part time job in retail. Despite my state of mind, I called them and they graciously offered me twelve to seventeen hours a week. This was something at least. It left a lot of free time in which fear, anxiety and depression maintained its hold on me. I could not recover from the fact that instead of rising to the challenge of my new position as property manager, I had fallen into an abyss.

Throughout this time I continued to go to the local chapel to pray in front of the Blessed Sacrament. I grew up going to mass every Sunday and although I had abandoned that practice, I continued to visit the chapel regularly for twelve years. While growing up, I was taught that Jesus was present in the Blessed Sacrament. The Blessed Sacrament is best described as being gold in color: a circle depicting the host, with rays emanating from it. It is the consecrated host. I was taught that the priest changes the elements of bread into the body of Christ. This is what we call the host. The Blessed Sacrament is a structural symbol of this. It is placed on the altar. I believed that Jesus was present in the Blessed Sacrament and desired to visit him and receive healing from him.

I am using past tense because I have begun meditating, and I have discovered the peace of directly communing with God through a meditation technique called Kriya Yoga, which I will describe more fully later. I still go to the chapel and—now to mass—but my immediate source of strength lies in meditation. However, during this difficult time and throughout the years before discovering meditation, the chapel brought me immense comfort, and I believe I received healing there. I continue to go there regularly and find immeasurable peace in being able to meditate there.

Some things are more easily felt than explained. I believe that Truth speaks to your heart. I only know that at this chapel, when the Blessed Sacrament is not exposed, I experience only the calm of the chapel. However, when it is placed on the altar, I walk in and feel a tangible lightness in my soul; I feel a deep desire to connect with the God who provides us with the opportunity to know him. The mystery of it all can only be described as profound. Again, this connection started at the chapel and now continues and flourishes with meditation.

Throughout the period of leaving a job and starting a new one, these visits continued to be regular. I have to say that at times I dragged myself there to kneel in front of Jesus. Inside I felt a sense of hopelessness and was losing faith, but I prayed. I knew that God was hearing my prayers but I was not completely trusting that he would answer them.

After several weeks of part-time employment my feeling of hitting bottom had not dissipated. I floundered, proceeding clumsily and in confusion for several weeks. I continued to battle with my demons of fear, anxiety and despair. At times these feelings permeated my being. I could not sleep or eat. Every hour of the day and night became an eternity. It was not the eternity of bliss I had contemplated after my earthly life was through, as God promises. I was living in hell. Every minute of every waking hour I experienced profound dread and hopelessness. Dread is that negative condition beyond fear. It is pure terror. For those of you who find yourself there, know that there is a way out.

With whatever will I had left, in combination with what I feel is God's grace, I began to get the newspaper each day and persevered in finding full-time employment. This, I have to say, is hard to do. For those of you who have been, or are in despair, you know what I mean. For me, reading the "Help Wanted" ads became more of a reminder of how many jobs I was not qualified to do. This was especially discouraging because I had worked steadily for nearly twenty years.

I had begun working in my early twenties. I was studying Art History in college and was close to getting my Bachelor of Arts degree. I had difficulty making school a priority and soon found myself suspended for a semester. I began to look for work and found a job through a temporary job placement agency. Soon I became system administrator of the company. I enjoyed financial freedom and independence, while receiving respect for my intelligence. I decided that school was not important and did not try to go back. I remained gainfully employed until the company was bought out. Then I was asked to stay on as a consultant for a few weeks; I was the only one in the company who understood the computer system and the reports it could produce for the new CEO. After that, it was not long until I found employment again.

This time I started temporary work in data entry, and soon was hired full time as the material coordinator of the company. I purchased all the parts for the ovens for which we manufactured soldered circuit boards. I had my own office and again was quite satisfied, but soon a recession—particularly in the high-tech industry—affected my career. I was let go.

Gratefully, I was able to work in purchasing again in my family's business and remained there for six years. I also wrote to the University that had suspended me and requested re-entry with the encouragement of my parents. I had to convince the school that I was ready to go back. I had to get straight As in my two remaining classes to get my degree. I focused and did it, while working, receiving a B.A. in Art History.

After that I got married, had two children and stayed home with them, working part-time nights and weekends in a local museum and in retail until they were school age. When my children entered school, I applied for the before mentioned assistant property manager/leasing consultant position, and then the job that I walked away from.

I felt that because I had accumulated what I considered to be a wealth of work experience, I would be able to find a job that matched what I was seeking. Instead I felt more despair. It was as if everything employers were looking for was something I could not provide. Still, I answered many ads and sent out countless resumes, persevering despite rejection. There were some wonderful part-time opportunities where I interviewed and got the job, but soon realized it was not what I was looking for.

# MIRACULOUS

One day in late March 2004, I responded to an ad for a receptionist who would assist the property managers. I was still in a state of mental despair. It took all my strength to force myself even to purchase the newspaper that day. I was so tired of circling ads, sending out letters and resumes, and feeling let down. This ad provided a phone number. I called. The person answering the phone sounded welcoming. She suggested that I come in and fill out an application. I pulled my feeble feeling self together and went.

Looking back on it, the experience seems surreal. I had all but crumbled inside, yet being inside of that office I felt a spark of my old self and hope. I filled out the application and was disappointed that I could not interview with the owner immediately. Since I had barely gotten it together to go there, waiting only prolonged my torture. The owner called the next day after reading my resume and application, and asked me to come in for an interview. After the interview, I was hired.

Writing about this, even now, brings out so many emotions. It is hard to describe the experience I have had since being hired by this company. The owner and his wife merit their employees' dedication. My coworkers are a mix of incredibly wonderful people. I have been provided with the opportunity to grow and feel supported in the new challenges my job offers me.

Back then, I had lost faith in my ability as a career woman, but was beginning to regain it. Fortunately, my faith in my ability to be a good mom has never been a question. Faith in my abilities as an artist emerged in 1992—for a while. With the security of my work environment and the never-ending joy of motherhood, I came into a place mentally and spiritually to be able to look at that part of my life that had emerged twelve years ago.

# INNER VISIONS

In 1992, my life at work was fine. I was single and living alone in an apartment in a new city. I was feeling isolated at home and I began to feel increasing despair about my loneliness and felt like expressing it through painting. During many lonely hours after work and on weekends, I thought about my desire to paint. Many accumulated years of pent up emotions wanted expression—frustration about my life, heartbreak, lost jobs, all those different things we experience in our twenties.

I went to the local art store and purchased various watercolor and acrylic paints, watercolor paper and brushes. I knew only that I had a deep desire to paint. What, I knew not. I had obtained my B.A. in Art History because I had a love of art. Drawing 101 and 102 were part of the curriculum, but, I had never taken a painting class. One evening, in my apartment with music playing, I poured color after color on a paper plate, set out paper and brushes on a towel on the carpet, and with a cup of water, I began.

The first painting that poured out of me was *Wounded Lioness* (Figure 1); this was in June of 1992. This painting represents the expression of my state of mind at that time. Also I identify with the astrological sign of Leo, the lion. This painting represents my emotions at a time when I felt beat up by the world. We come into the world as infants, innocent and joyful by nature. I feel that we all get worn down at a certain point through our conditioning and interacting with society. Youthful ideals don't match reality. My depiction of this wounded lioness, where there is a hazy look to one eye and a steely look to the other, reflects back to me the dichotomy of the human spirit, where we are at once defeated, yet strong. There is a sense in this work of being wounded, yet it contains a sense of resolve to persevere. We are beaten, but not broken; this is the theme.

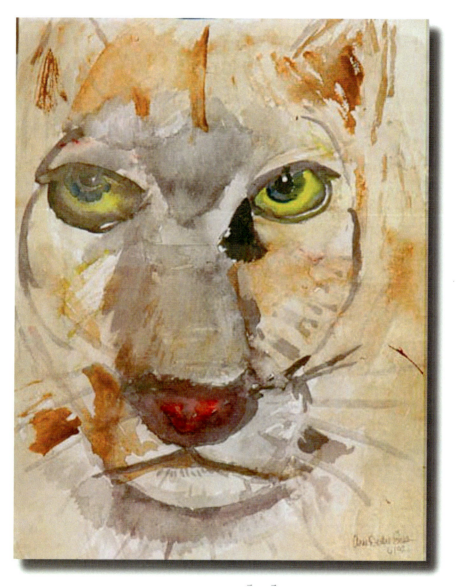

Figure 1: Wounded Lioness

With this first painting completed, I was overwhelmed by the joy of having captured my feelings. Suddenly it didn't matter if I never felt good enough in school art class. I had my own measure of what I considered good. I had expressed myself. It was the beginning. Soon I longed to paint. I painted day after day, after work. And in the solitude of my apartment, I no longer felt quite so all alone.

The next illustration was created a month later. Titled *Calm After the Storm* (Figure 2), I chose to include it in this book for several reasons. It was a painting that would not die. I saturated the paper with water and paint—actually folded it in half to create the two palm trees—in a subconscious risk taking state. This painting proved to me that I could go to the point of almost ruining it, by taking the risk of folding it in half without knowing how the painting would unfold. This painting showed me that if an image was meant to emerge it would, no matter what risks I took as an artist to create it. It was really a turning point for me. I had been painting steadily since *Wounded Lioness*.

Works included *Light at the End of the Tunnel, Eucalyptus Leaves, Spiritual Roses,* and others. But *Calm After the Storm* showed me an element of guidance at work. No matter how many risks I took, the painting emerged soundly. This is something I remind myself of now: TRUST! It is meant to be. This means allowing things to happen. I call it God's guiding hand at work.

Later that month came *Inner Vision* (Figure 3). This is the first representation of connecting to my spiritual self—my Pure Self. It represents the third eye of intuition. Understanding intuition has burgeoned into a spiritual insight I never thought possible. Most people are aware of gut feelings and perhaps acknowledge it as their own intuition. I feel it is more than that. Jesus said that the kingdom of God is within you.

Figure 2: Calm After the Storm

There is a Divine consciousness which we all can access through the Holy Spirit.

In this painting there are gray lines underneath the eye. The beauty of gray is something I was exploring. The beauty of gray is an idea that says: Beyond where I think I am right and you are wrong, is the truth. The ego will defend it's position and create a false sense of rightness—one that makes the other person wrong. This creates hatred, intolerance and violence. These negative emotions can be felt by all of us, but it is important when in conflict with someone that you try to see their point of view. We all have egos, but we each also have a Divine Soul—the Pure Self.

Balance is important and something I am achieving after many years of going to extremes: at times self-destructive, and at times health conscious. I have made peace with my demons. I read about Buddha who sat under the Boddhi tree; when the demons came he did not run from them and he did not get angry with them. He invited them to sit with him.

Jesus said to love your enemies. Sometimes the enemies lie inside of you, and to have peace you must forgive yourself and forgive others; love yourself and love others. Your ego condemns you and others, but stronger inside you is your Pure Self. We are not our own gods, but rather come from God, and heaven is inside us when we remember that. Meditation facilitates this process.

*Inner Vision* is one of my first spiritually revealing paintings. I titled the book Inner Visions because I became conscious of the collection of paintings I had done that became spiritual revelations to me in visual form.

I painted *Thirst—the Soul is a Spiritual Garden* (Figure 4) in December 1992. It took me approximately four hours, and during those four hours, I

Figure 3: Inner Vision

truly painted from an internal source. I felt guided during the process. After assembling the colors and picking up the paintbrush, I remember little more than a voice within me directing my brush strokes. I finished the piece and promptly named it.

It was only recently that I came to understand the meaning of the title. For *Thirst*, I found a Bible quote: *To him that thirsteth, I will give the fountain of the water of life, freely* (Apocalypse of St. John the Apostle 21:6). *Garden*, in the title, represents that sacred place inside of you, a sanctuary that is eternal. There are three flowers in the painting, representing the trinity of Father, Son and Holy Spirit. There is a baptismal quality to this painting. Jesus promised to be with us always through the gift of the Holy Spirit, which nourishes your soul. This is depicted through the rain falling on the flowers.

In *The Complete Floral Healer* by Anne McIntyre, she describes the meaning behind flowers. In this painting, the flowers resemble chrysanthemums. In her book, chrysanthemums symbolize connecting to the spiritual self, and less with the ephemeral, temporal aspect of life. This painting helps me to remember that when we thirst for God's truth, we begin to remember His gift of the Holy Spirit within us, which is an eternal spring where we thirst no more.

In John, Chapter 4, Jesus talks with the Samaritan woman near a well. He asks her for a drink of water. He states: *Whosoever drinketh of this water, shall thirst again; but he that shall drink of the water that I will give him, shall not thirst for ever: But the water that I will give him shall become in him a fountain of water, springing up into life everlasting* (verse 13–14).

I painted *Roses in a Mist of Pink* (Figure 5) in May of 1993. I had just given my mother a hanging basket of flowers for Mother's Day. This was the inspiration for this piece. After painting it, I saw the spiritual essence

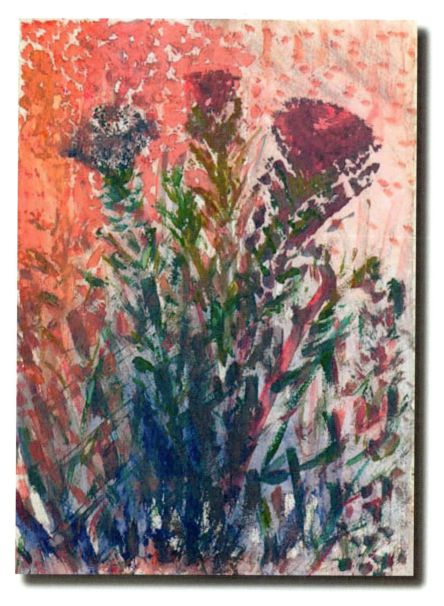

Figure 4: Thirst—The Soul is a Spiritual Garden

Figure 5: Roses in a Mist of Pink

of it. It represents connecting to the Blessed Mother, our Eternal Mother who is always watching out for us. The misty quality of the background reminds me of our eternal home—I believe that we are spiritual beings in a physical world.

A few months later, in August of 1993, came *Mother Mary* (Figure 6). I remember feeling grateful for her guidance and wanted, with all my heart, to paint the glory of God. Mary's willingness to obey God is admirable, and through her purity and trust in God, we have Jesus.

The sun in this painting is depicted as a rose, which symbolizes Mary, and the celestial heavens opened up to us through her son, Jesus. The gift that Christ gives us is eternal life. Jesus promised to never leave us, and gave us the Holy Spirit to dwell with us. Jesus' life and death were about forgiveness and unconditional love. When we connect to that we are capable of experiencing heaven on Earth. The power of love and forgiveness can heal and transform the planet and all beings.

The following year, I painted *White Roses* (Figure 7) in October of 1994. My interest in art and interior design inspired the subject matter: a vase of flowers on a table. The contemporary table with scroll base came from an image in my mind. The white roses symbolize purity in love—a love that is eternal and unconditional. I have an image of loved ones who have passed away and believe that they would send us white roses as a token of their timeless love for us as we struggle here on Earth, much like our living loved ones send us flowers on special occasions or during difficult times.

Winter in New England has sometimes been a dark time for me. In December of 1994, I painted *Winter Flowers* (Figure 8). The feeling of hope inspired this. These flowers are colorful and light in essence despite the snow falling around them. There is a saying that Hope springs eternal. Even in a winter storm, when we remember God's love we find hope.

Figure 6: Mother Mary

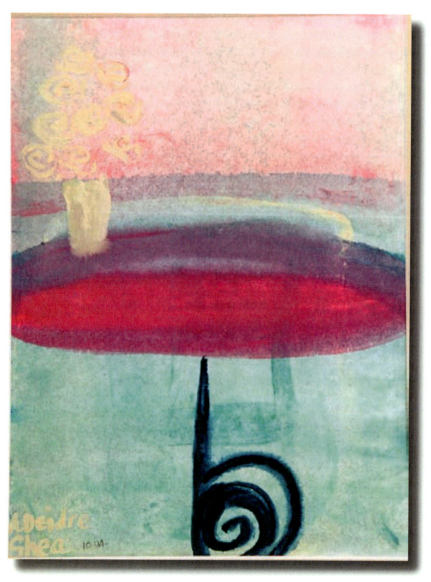

Figure 7: White Roses

Figure 8: Winter Flowers

In January of 1995, I painted *Blue Water* (Figure 9). This painting was inspired by the idea of travel. It depicts a terrace, perhaps a view from a home in Europe—more specifically Italy. I think terraces are a wonderful way to experience the outdoors while at home. I believe that being in nature, especially close to water, is healing. The wild pink roses climbing the wrought iron fence are another element from the outdoors that is integrated into the home environment. This painting reminds me to spend time in nature, as it is essential to healing and one's wellbeing. It also reminds me that there are many wonderfully diverse cultures, and to travel and experience them is good for the soul.

In March of 1995, I began to question the attachments I had to behaviors that took me outside of myself, like having a few drinks and shopping—the usual diversions when you are trying to escape yourself and the world before realizing your Divine Source. *Serenity* (Figure 10) was painted at that time and is powerful to me now, because I came to understand it later. Like most of my paintings I feel that it came from an internal source and was guided. I chose the colors; the visual image appeared after several hours.

I have come to understand the importance of meditation. The visual depiction of the painting Serenity is about meditation. It consists of a background that transforms from blue tones to light yellow/white. In meditation, as we connect to God, we go through a process of earthly connections or thoughts, depicted as the flowers and leaves floating in the piece. We begin to watch their intensity diminish until we reach clarity of mind—represented by the light or candle at the upper right corner of the painting.

Meditation is crucial to our connecting with our source, God, the Creator. He lives within us, and through our intuition is always speaking to

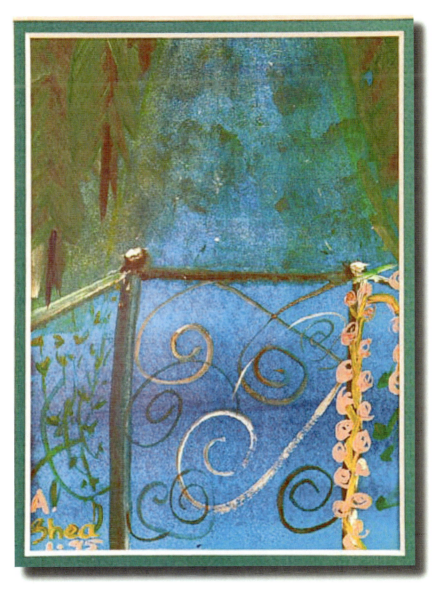

Figure 9: Blue Water

Figure 10: Serenity

us, whispering, quietly guiding. It is important to learn to quiet your mind, your ego voice, and listen to and experience the voice of true love inside your Pure Self. When you experience this you will know without a doubt that you are never alone. And you will experience a peace of mind that is indescribable.

*Pansies* (Figure 11) was painted later in March of 1995. It is more detailed because I drew it in pencil first, inspired by a flower calendar that I had. Because it was not an inner vision that I had, I interpret it differently. In *The Complete Floral Healer*, author Anne McIntyre describes the essence of pansies. I find spiritual truths relevant to this description. In her book she connects pansies to the healing of heartbreak.

Most people do not go through life without experiencing heartbreak. It is inherent to attachment. Unconditional love is the solution to this painful state. Unconditional love does not depend on whether someone loves you back or meets any expectations you may have. It is liberating to love and be loved in a relationship founded on trust, communication and accepting the other person, loving without controlling or placing limits on them. This is a purer form of love. God's unconditional love for us teaches us how to love others.

Doubt and control affect love and create heartbreak. A lot of heartbreak is unnecessary. Being aware of your ego helps—that it wants what it wants. Ego is the source of desires and experiences pain. Higher love—accepting—frees you from this pain. Unconditional love is given freely without the expectation of getting anything in return. This is the highest level of love.

Several years went by before I had the inclination to paint again. In May of 1999, as summer was approaching, I felt the season changing in my soul. I painted *Summer Pinks and Greens* (Figure 12). It had been four

Figure 11: Pansies

years since my last painting and I began to feel, wondrously, filled with color and the desire to capture the essence of that feeling through painting. I felt the colors of pink and green, purchased these colors at my local art store, along with a large piece of watercolor paper. I remember feeling excited about the lime green color I purchased because it was metallic. I also got a tube of white acrylic paint and silver metallic acrylic paint. I knew without a doubt, at the paint store, that I would be able to express my inner connection through the essence of these colors and I was filled with joy.

Before I paint, I often feel the colors. When I saw that there were metallic hues available I connected with them. To me, metallic paints can enhance the feeling of the work. It is a subtle shimmer that accents. In terms of feeling, and being filled with the desire to communicate that effervescent quality, I was excited to experiment with the metallic hues. After painting *Summer Pinks and Greens,* I was not let down. I feel that the colors reflect what I felt inside.

Regarding subject matter, as usual, I did not know what would come through. It represents two wonderfully different dichotomies expressed in one painting. At the right is a free-standing calla lily arrangement. Calla lilies represent purity, order and the Divine. There is more of a sense of restraint and attention to detail. On the left is a flourish of leaves with a single pink flower. I let go and felt unrestrained while painting the vine-like leaves and flower. Close to both are white scroll leaf designs. I felt a lot of energy going from the bottom of the paper towards the top as if in a spiraling motion upward. The beauty of this work for me is it's combination of the wild and the restrained—embracing both of these qualities within myself—along with the vivid color of lime green with metallic shimmer as the background of surprise.

The next painting is emotional for me. This is the painting that proved to the doubting part of me that I could paint. It was September of 1999, and I had recently gone back to work part-time as my children were still very young. I got a job working at the world-renowned Currier Museum of Art. The people there were amazing. I was thrilled to be working there, as I was finally doing something in my field, Art History.

Spending time at the museum, I began to think about my formal education in the arts. Difficult as it was for me to write, read and memorize several hundred paintings and pass exams to gain that degree, my interest was there. I connected as early as high school to the realization that art throughout the ages was a beautifully revealing visual representation of time throughout history. It helped bring life to the texts I was reading about the history of our world. An example of this is found in the glorious cathedrals throughout the world. People worked day and night to build these monuments to God, creating beautiful stained glass works of art to illuminate some of these buildings. They were divinely inspired to glorify God.

To fulfill the curriculum during high school and while pursuing my degree, I had taken beginning classes in studio art. This consisted primarily of drawing. My experience in these classes was not very positive. I definitely did not feel "good enough," and never went further than beginning drawing, not even trying painting classes, which were upper level classes. The painting I did in September of 1999, *Inspired* (Figure 13), means so much to me because it helped me break free and gain confidence in an inward way.

I had been painting on my own for seven years, but working at the Currier made me think about taking a formal painting class. I was so excited about this idea that I called and requested a catalog from a local

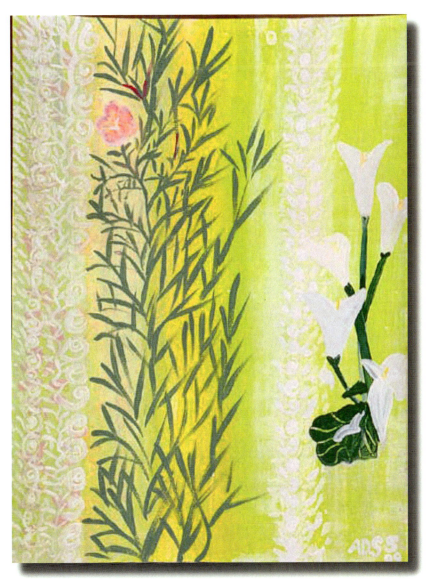

Figure 12: Summer Pinks and Greens

Figure 13: Inspired

institute which offered art classes. The catalog arrived and I began looking for an evening class to accommodate my stay-at-home mom schedule. Reading through the catalog, I discovered that there were not any painting classes that would work with my schedule. I felt devastation deep within that is hard to describe. I had been painting on my own for some time but at that moment I felt that I needed a class to make it real. Could I be an artist without a formal painting class? At that moment, I felt I needed a class, and all my hopes crumbled when I realized it was not possible to take one.

Feeling very sad, that evening, I decided to sit out on my deck in the late summer air and paint my disappointment. I sat down, assembled my paints, and began. My paintings usually begin with color selection and building up the background. This is always a process of letting go. I paint; I wipe away with a paper towel, paint, clear away, and so on. This may take several hours. When the background feels right, I begin painting the image. With *Inspired*, I again felt guided. What came through after several hours astonished me, because I had told myself, "You can't paint without first taking a painting class." The fact that I was not able to take the class, but painted satisfactorily despite this, was very meaningful for me. I learned a lesson in trust once again.

So, what if I couldn't take the class? This painting made me feel happy, joyful and inspired despite what I had thought was a setback. Classes may be beneficial, but are not necessarily required, even if it's something that you want to do. I titled this painting *Inspired*, because to be inspired means to be "in spirit;" it comes from within not the outside. You can connect with this truth.

The next painting, *Timeless Love*, (Figure 14) is a visual reminder to me that perfect love is not only the one truth we bring into the afterlife; it is also the truth of who we really are. It is our Pure Self. On Earth we are surrounded by the illusion of material comforts, or their lack. Meanwhile, we hear, "You can't take it with you."

Throughout our earthly lives we often feel compelled to strive for greater material success. The truth is, money cannot buy happiness. We all know how good it feels to purchase something we like, but really this is often just a temporary high. We often end up collecting clutter, which leads to a sense of crowding, disorganization and actual soul heaviness. We can end up living with too much stuff and then having yard sales. Donating these extra items to local charities is wonderful; also you can live simply and determine which charities—local or overseas—to donate to directly, without buying the extra stuff.

The actual process of painting *Timeless Love* has a lot to do, again, with being guided. As I was working with the watercolors, they formed this image with very little brush stroke work from me. Of note are the rainbow colors coming out from the bottom of the vase. These colors just came together like that on their own—as did much of the blue atmospheric background.

Two books I highly recommend are Norman Paulsen's *Sacred Science: Meditation, Transformation, Illumination*, and Paramahansa Yogananda's *The Second Coming of Christ—The Resurrection of the Christ Within You*. I have learned to appreciate this painting through spiritual eyes and have learned from these books about the rainbow pathway to God. These books refer to a Kriya Yoga meditation technique, which I now practice and highly recommend. Through study and meditation, I have come to realize the value of letting go of a materialistic way of thinking. Matter and materialism weighs us down. Love uplifts and transforms us. We know this at heart and meditation is a practice that helps us realize the blissful state that is meant to be our true reality. God is a loving parent, and through

Figure 14: Timeless Love

meditation—that is, by directly communing with God—we are able to realize and experience our Pure Self of love, which is eternal, connected to all of creation, and most importantly connected to our Creator.

When we are in the throes of our daily lives—working hard, acquiring—we don't see the vicious cycle we are in. The rainbow path to God shows us a way towards true freedom. Pure love is endless, timeless and lasting. Experience this and you will experience the truest freedom and joy, instead of the hollowness of chasing after temporary fixes.

Meditation is a process whereby we don't have to give things up all at once. But rather, like a truly loving parent, God gently helps us to discover the lasting benefits of detachment. Through this process we become eager to let go—we can feel a sense of liberation. It is a gentle, gradual process.

Later that same month I painted *Café* (Figure 15) This piece came out so differently than I had anticipated when I sat down on my deck to paint it. As I described with *Blue Water*, I like the integrating of indoors and out—meaning decks and terraces. The idea I had for this painting was to create a café scene. I envisioned a lush garden setting surrounding wrought iron chairs and tables, filled with restaurant patrons enjoying fine cuisine and conversation. In my mind, I saw a lot of greenery with flowering plants surrounding the outdoor café, like you would see in Europe.

After several hours, I completed the work and was surprised to see the image that came through. This painting showed me that despite my intentions, the truth of where I was would prevail. Through the gray, gloomy atmosphere and single table and chair in the painting—not the many tables and chairs filled with happy customers—I am expressing the solitude and loneliness I was feeling at the time. The vase of flowers on the table, however, powerfully asserts to me that spirit of overcoming. To

Figure 15: Café

overcome is to prevail. Your Pure Self will always prevail, just as God through Jesus has conquered all darkness. "In the world you shall have distress but have confidence, I have overcome the world" (John 16:33). This is the true gift that Jesus has given to all of us. Through the Holy Spirit, which he gave to us through his death, we find the Spirit of everlasting life which contains the end of our suffering.

Jesus promised that he would always be with us. Jesus keeps his promises. He told his disciples: "You are the light of the world." (Matthew 5:14). Through his life and death he overcame the world. Not only that but he gave us his Spirit in order for us to do the same. As lights or light workers for God, we can all partake in sharing the light on Earth. The world is filled with temptations that constantly distract us from our Pure Self, which is love. But Jesus overcame the world. He didn't battle his enemies with hatred, for he said: "Father, forgive them, for they know not what they do." (St. Luke 23:34) Jesus did not conquer through violence, but rather, through mercy, forgiveness and love. These are the most powerful forces on Earth.

To be merciful, forgiving and loving, we must begin with ourselves. Intellectually we know this. To truly experience this reality, each one of us, every day, can start by saying to ourselves "I forgive myself" and mean it. We all deserve mercy. Truly being kind, forgiving, merciful and loving with ourselves may seem uncomfortable at first. I don't think that we are brought up or conditioned to believe that we deserve this. If you think about it, judgments of ourselves and of others becomes ingrained—habitual. Realize this does not come forth from reality. Know this because Jesus came to Earth to tell us this. This is not just something that happened long ago. We can experience heaven on Earth now if we forgive ourselves and live in virtue.

It is true liberation from the limitations of our egos that God longs for us to experience. When you practice forgiving yourself throughout each day you begin to experience peace. Your ego may tell you that you don't deserve it. But gently embrace your dark feelings, which are not of your Pure Self, and know that your true birthright is joy. When you forgive yourself you can begin to forgive others; from forgiveness stems compassion and liberation not only for yourself but for everyone. In that way heaven is not a destination, but an experience now while we are on Earth.

The next painting came a month later: *Sunrise* (Figure 16). This image is a depiction of our path toward enlightenment. If we would remember from birth until our earthly death our one Pure Self of Love there would be no need for us to follow the path of enlightenment—we would already be enlightened. I believe that we are born blissful, loving beings. However, throughout the process of being in the world we lose sight of that. We can ignorantly choose to follow the path of destruction because we forget who we really are.

God, out of his love for us gave us all free will. How true could love be if it was forced upon us? God does not force us to love him. This proves his love for us. He loves us enough to give us free will—a choice. Because he is the omniscient ruler of creation, he allows Satan to exist. He knows that eventually we all come to realize the lies inherent in Satan's nature. We hear "learn the hard way." Most of us experience this.

Sometimes it can take a while to acknowledge that we are choosing not to love, but rather judge, condemn and hurt others. This really does not feel good and we don't see a way out of it. We blame ourselves, blame others and create a vicious cycle. The way out of this is to forgive yourself. We hear "Love yourself, then you can love someone else." That is all right

Figure 16: Sunrise

intellectually, but experiencing it can be uncomfortable. The painting Sunrise is a depiction of the idea of waking up to a new day—starting over. After we have had our fill of self-inflicted condemnations or through experiencing that from others, we are ready to experience something better.

During the process of creating this work, the watercolors formed the path towards the sun with little effort from me. This path represents our way home. It is our birthright to find our way home. When you become aware that such a path exists, you begin following it. This is your path to liberation. On it, you will discover that your Pure Self is immune to other's criticisms or opinions of you. This is freeing. You become focused on following this path because you are connecting to the energy and source of creation.

You begin to experience a power greater than material wealth— you are experiencing spiritual riches, spiritual gold, spiritual wisdom. When you are on the path to enlightenment, through experience, study and meditation you gain wisdom. This is not knowledge—facts you have learned in your academic career. I would like to see our educational system more focused on the spirit of our youths than anything else.

Having material wealth is not in itself bad, but recognizing that your spirit—the Pure Self—is more important than anything money can buy is endlessly beneficial. Practicing virtue is vital on the road towards enlightenment. Again, we are all born knowing our Pure Self, but through free will choices we forget. When we remember, and begin our journey home, each day becomes ripe with possibilities. As illusory veils become lifted, we see the path towards the ultimate freedom of existence. We seldom see this path in the midst of our busy daily lives. However, think of those times when you were kind to someone. Remember how good you felt. This is the spark of remembering your blissful Pure Self.

Virtues such as charity, faith, loyalty, patience, honesty, perseverance, temperance, humility, courage, equanimity, continence and compassion, as described in *Sacred Science* by Norman Paulsen, all facilitate this path towards freedom. Along with practicing these virtues, it is recommended to follow a path of equilibrium, and balancing of recreation, work, nourishment, association, speech, study, conduct and meditation. I highly recommend this book.

A few days later, I painted *Peaceful* (Figure 17). Another name that comes to me regarding this work is *A Glimpse of Heaven*. To be peaceful is to reach a state of tranquility—an absence of war—inner contentment. Jesus said: "Peace I leave with you, my peace I give unto you." (John 14:27) We may have heard these words in church. The purpose of this book is to help you connect to this reality and experience it fully for yourself, not just as a platitude. The feeling you will have upon truly experiencing this state for yourself will convince you without a doubt of the meaning of your life. This is a permanent, authentic knowing unlike that experienced from the temporary high of acquiring something material. By material, I mean all things subject to decay—temporary things. This relates to addictions as well.

Inner peace comes through meditation. Meditation may be uncomfortable at first. We believe that we don't have the time, or that we are not going to get anything out of it, so why bother. Bother, because it is your direct link to the God who created everything. I understand that this may not seem important to some people. Our everyday lives seem to have taken over all our thoughts and time, and it seems like we're doing all right on our own. But, realize that when we think we are doing all right on our

Figure 17: Peaceful

Figure 18: Dream of Giverny

own, we might be relying on alcohol, medications or other drugs and caffeine to get by. Meditation—stilling the mind—following Kriya Yoga meditation, as described in Sacred Science, can reveal much to us.

Let God guide you. My experience was that of changing from a feeling of running on empty to now running more often on full. I have more work to do. However, I am feeling enough benefit from living more spiritually to say that I prefer this natural energy to other means—it is constantly refreshing and renewing. To intellectually know something is one thing; to experience it is something else. Someone can tell you something and you know you should, but you have to try it on your own and see for yourself the mysterious and powerful energy of the universe found in peaceful meditation. It is amazing—a gift you give to yourself. It will renew your mind, body and spirit, and give your life new purpose.

Several months later, I painted *Dream of Giverny* (Figure 18). My friend Michelle helped me name this work since I had been inspired by Monet's *Water Lilies*, and did not want to duplicate that name. Water lilies represent to me in a visual way the survival instinct. We hear: *Sink or swim*; water lilies represent that instinct to swim. They are beautiful in their ability to transcend the element of water—that element which has the power to heal as well as the power to drown. Personally, I connect to both experiences. My Pure Self, as well as yours, can overcome.

Throughout my life, I had felt myself drowning metaphorically. With my spiritual eyes now open, I see a way out that is permanent and a source of endless strength. However, I am grateful for the experiences that brought me to that drowning place since I have, through faith, swum my way back to the air, finding the light, overcoming the darkness. I believe this is relevant because there are those of us who do not swim, but sink—those who commit suicide physically, emotionally, mentally or spiritually.

This is a reality where there is darkness, and the light of God, present in all of us, is not recognized. This is a tragedy. When we are sinking, most of us don't realize the negative impact of it on our daily lives. We shop, drink alcohol, take drugs, seek entertainment and have various less-than-fulfilling relationships and continue on in hopes of filling the void.

Those who sink further see only despair and no way out. They kill themselves to alleviate the pain. All of the above mentioned means of self-medicating no longer work. The tragedy of this is that within all of those who choose to end their lives, there is a light of hope within them. They became disconnected from that and have lost faith. I have come close to this state of mind. *Dream of Giverny* is about remembering this faith, which is survival at its core, raw core, where we swim, when all we have left to hold on to is our faith.

My mother recently told me that the one thing that my dad, who passed away nearly four years ago, wanted me to have was faith. Coming as close to "drowning" as I have, I am grateful for the faith they have instilled in me. It is my hope to pass it on to others.

Later that month, December 1999, I painted *Lit from Within* (Figure 19). I am as susceptible as anyone who lives in a wintry climate to the feeling of being overwhelmed from the cold, dark and seemingly endlessness of winter. This painting depicts the spirit of overcoming such feelings. It is a momentous ray of upward moving brush strokes, a bright pink background, a purple rose at its center, along with yellow and light pink flowers joining in the feeling of being lit from within.

When I look at this painting, I am reminded of that important element of energy: light. Light is instrumental to our well-being. Being lit from within requires connecting to the universal energy of God. Light energy is relevant in terms of health. Think of Reiki healing. This is a

Figure 19: Lit From Within

healing energy that Reiki healers can transmit to us, and we can draw into ourselves. We are beings of light energy. Connecting to God through meditation provides us with this energy to function at our highest level. When we disconnect from our source, we lose our natural, lasting energy, and have to rely on alternative, temporary means.

Two years went by and I had come to a place where I was not connecting to God on a regular basis. This is depicted in *Faith* (Figure 20), October, 2001. The true meaning of this painting is faith. Whether this is something my father instilled in me, or I gained by grace, or both, the reality of it remains constant. I do not say lightly that I recommend to those of us who are influencing our children that we provide to them a belief and trust in God—faith.

This painting depicts a time in my life when I was being swallowed up by a despair of my own making. It is simple in it's depiction. The rose represents our true spirit of love, the Pure Self. As God gave us free will, during the time that I painted *Faith*, I was drowning in an abyss of self-inflicted agony. I was choosing to see the glass half empty instead of half full. I see that now in retrospect, but the feeling of an all-pervading gloom surrounded me—like the concentric circles in the painting—trying to choke me.

I am grateful for the dark times, because they have urged me inevitably towards the light, although, during the experience of dark times, it is as though that is all there is. Looking back, I was close to losing faith, a feeling I have struggled with before, losing connection with my Pure Self. I now realize the poverty of the soul that can ensue from looking outside of yourself for happiness. I do not blame myself, or society. It is pure ignorance. I was not aware of a different reality in that moment of time.

Figure 20: Faith

Figure 21: Divine Mercy, Resurrection

# INNER VISIONS

In this world, we are constantly bombarded with so-called opportunities to feel better. Looked at closely, they are opportunities that are outside of ourselves. I tried those methods and came up bankrupt within myself. This is depicted in the painting. I was in that state of looking outside of myself for happiness and was neglecting to nourish myself from the inside, from connecting to God who would provide me with a lasting source of nourishment. We are all born knowing the powerful connection we have to God, but because I was forgetting this, I began to drown. It was the beginning of a tumultuous time for me as I struggled to find my path back home.

Back to the beginning of my story: three years later, through faith, I found my way back to my dream. I didn't think that I had a dream and didn't know where to begin to form one. *Divine Mercy, Resurrection* (Figure 21), subtitled *Violet Flame*, was the beginning for me to remember and to connect to what was always there. At 7:30 pm, which was early for me in terms of painting, I told myself to sit down, assemble my paints, and begin. That was November 2004. I had painted a few times in the past several years but did not feel as satisfied from the experience as I had previously. I had begun to lose a little hope. What I realize now is that God's time is not always my time. Those little exercises when I felt that I was not successful in painting were indeed successful in their pure expression. Expecting the perfect outcome every time I sit down to paint is not realistic. "Just see what happens" is my new motto.

But in November 2004, I painted for six and a half hours. That was monumental for me, in terms of the amount of energy I had. Initially I sat down at 7:30 thinking I would give it a try. At 2:00 a.m., I was overwhelmed with gratitude. Even upon waking later, it felt like Christmas morning. My doubts about myself dissolved.

# MIRACULOUS

This painting represents the Trinity—One God in combination with the Son and the Holy Spirit. The rays emanating from the heart of the flower depict mercy. The violet colors in it reflect the violet flame, which is said to transmute negative energy into positive energy. This is a powerful energy we can assimilate and use to transform ourselves and help others.

We are constantly bombarded with negativity. The key to transmuting this energy is to sincerely want the best for others. When others are negative towards us, have compassion; listen and realize the power of understanding where they are coming from. Through understanding we can facilitate healing on many levels. So-called difficult people really just need to be heard. Hear them, understand, and sincerely communicate to them that you are listening, and you can avoid conflict.

Also that evening, I painted *Purity of Love*, which is so light in color that it does not print well. Translating my concept of true love into a symbolic painting helped affirm my belief in the power of love. It is a vase of white roses, on a white table, with an Ionic order column as a table base.

I looked up "Ionic order" in the dictionary after I painted it, realizing it was a specific order (as opposed to Doric or Corinthian in Greek architecture). Its spiral scroll-shaped ornaments differentiate it. Spirals connect heaven to Earth. This was suitable in terms of the meaning of the painting. I also looked up "ions." Ions attract negative energy—dirt—and purify it, much like an air purifier in your home. I realized the Ionic order column symbolized this purity along with the white roses and white background.

Six and a half hours of painting—after years had gone by—helped me to remember a joy in life I had forgotten. We are all given a gift to help us connect to our spirituality. I know as well as anyone that having a gift does not necessarily mean that you will acknowledge it. I know now that we are all given gifts and to connect to them can provide an endless source of joy. This is a gift from God to all of us. Maybe it is your sense of humor that can lighten other's hearts, or kindness, or the ability to listen. We are provided with opportunities in our daily lives to simply, yet meaningfully, improve the lives of others and as a side result, improve our own life. Many of us may feel a calling towards the creative arts. Stay connected with God through meditation and you will know no limits.

Of equal importance is our attitude in dealing with people every day. Realize that reacting to anger with judgment and retribution will only bring you and others down. My emotions in those situations used to hit me like a truck and leave me for dead. Today things are different. I've learned that when someone is angry and I respond with anger, a negative downward spiral is created. Responding with understanding, not taking things personally, and desiring to dispel that anger through calm communication can uplift and transform the energy.

I first became aware of this while working in customer service jobs. When people came at me in anger and I got angry back at them, I noticed that it was a negative experience all around. One day, I decided to take myself out of the situation by mentally detaching from their anger. Instead, I began to listen to see how I could truly help them. I noticed that soon they became peaceful instead of aggressive, and I realized the benefit of compassionate listening.

The constant practice of vibrationally lifting negative energies within yourself and others, through love and forgiveness, is to transcend or rise above the mundane. It is a blissful state of mind. Each day presents many opportunities to practice this. The more you work to eliminate your own low level anger, jealousy and fear, the more resilient you are in the midst of these energies coming at you from other people. Eventually, they do not affect you, but rather flow on through you without causing you to react. If you change yourself so you do not resonate with base emotions, you will be fine no matter where you are or how many difficult people you encounter.

Jesus taught us this. Growing up Christian, I knew it intellectually. Through personal experience, reading and meditating, I now understand it more fully. This inspires my painting. I have a desire to make divinely inspired ideas or concepts visible. When I first began to paint, I wanted to express painful emotions, but as I continue to grow spiritually, I want to create powerful visual affirmations of universal truths—God's infinite mercy that flows into all of us. We are vessels of this mercy and have the opportunity every day to choose to acknowledge that love—that blessing—and pass it on to those around us: friends, family, loved ones and the people we briefly come in contact with throughout the day.

If you allow it, you absorb other people's negative energies, or low-level energies—anger, jealousy, etc.—whether it is aimed at you or just because you are around them. Be aware of the energies that you are carrying inside yourself. Through prayer, unconditional love and forgiveness you can dissipate or transform these energies in yourself and others, into higher level, positive ones.

A burning desire does not become extinguished even if you forget that it exists. It stays inside, perhaps purifying itself until it is ready to reemerge and you are able to recognize and deal with it.

We all have a mission; I believe that we all have deep aspirations. Go back to what you love—what gives you joy. Go back into childhood if you have to, and remember. Meditation and prayer facilitates this process.

There is something that you were meant to do and God put that spark inside of your soul. Ask him to help you connect with it. Prayer is talking to God; meditation is about listening to him.

I am reminded of Saint Matthew: "Not in bread alone doth man live, but in every word that proceedeth from the mouth of God." (4:4) Put God first. Without God keeping our hearts beating, our lungs breathing, our spirits in these bodies, we would not be here.

With that said, food, as support to the body can be medicinal. Cooking is a noble pursuit. Healthy cooking provides nourishment and fuels the body on a cellular level. And if you want to cook but feel that you can't, start simply. Find one recipe that appeals to you. Assemble the ingredients and go for it. This builds confidence and is a starting point for limitless creativity. Cooking healthy food and knowing what foods can provide you with your own unique source of light energy is beneficial.

It is important to have a positive outlet for accumulated energy. If you begin to lose your faith, you have to find your way back. I found myself drowning in my misery. Feeling no passion, I had to dig deep. In my spiritual quest I turned back to what I knew made me feel better, not realizing that it was my passion: discovering truth. Truth exists. We tell ourselves what we think truth is, but it is changeless. The spirit of truth exists regardless of our opinion. Light is stronger than darkness. Pure love elevates all conditions. Awareness of this activates higher levels of thinking and creates joy. My art is an attempt to express this in an image that can be understood by all.

In closing, the experience of the person who creates art and the one who views it can be similar if you are both connecting to the universal truth inherent in the art. Realize that you are pure love in your Pure Self, and acknowledge this truth. Forms of expression are true in their belief of this reality, whether expressing pain or joy. Emotional pain is a reality of choosing not to love. Choose to love and you will alter painful experiences. Love yourself; forgive yourself, this will help you to love others and forgive others. Know that the eternal sun is always shining behind the clouds.

In the New Testament, the holy city of Jerusalem is described coming down out of the heaven from God: And the city hath no need of the sun, nor of the moon, to shine in it. For the Glory of God hath enlightened it, and the Lamb is the lamp thereof (Apocalypse of St. John 21:23). The dueling natures which Jesus overcame are described in a quote from Rumi. When I told a friend of mine about the book I was writing she loaned me Painted Prayers, by Jody Uttal. This book is about an artist who interprets the spiritual wisdom of the masters. In it I found two noteworthy quotes. The first was from Rumi:

Out beyond ideas of wrongdoing and rightdoing, there is a field. I'll meet you there. When the soul lies down in that grass, the world is too full to talk about. Ideas, language, even the phrase 'each other' doesn't make sense.

The second wonderful quote is by Hafiz:

*I have learned so much from God that I can no longer call myself a Christian, a Hindu, a Muslim, a Buddhist, a Jew. The truth has shared so much of itself with me that I can no longer call myself a man, a woman, an angel or even pure soul. Love has befriended hafiz so completely it has turned to ash and freed me of every concept and image my mind has ever known.*

My hope is that you connect with the intent of this book, which is to always remember what Jesus told us: "The kingdom of heaven is at hand" (Matthew 4:17) within you, now.

# Resources

The Holy Bible, Translated from the Latin vulgate. James Cardinal Gibbons. Tan Books and Publishers, Inc. Rockford, IL. 1899 reprinted 1971.

McIntyre, Anne. *The Complete Floral Healer.* Sterling Publishing Co. New York, NY. 2002.

Paulsen, Norman. *Sacred Science: Meditation, Transformation, Illumination.* The Solar Logos Foundation. Sunburst Publishing. Buellton, CA. 2000.

Uttal, Jody. *Painted Prayers.* Tallfellow Press. Los Angeles, CA. 2002.

Yogananda, Paramahansa. T*he Second Coming of Christ: The Resurrection of the Christ Within You. Self-Realization Fellowship.* Los Angeles, CA. 2004.

# About the Author

Anne Deidre is a master intuitive and transformational leader, bestselling author, speaker, and spiritual teacher. Known as the "Intuitive Life Makeover and Book Coach," she facilitates powerful healing as she transmits Divine Energy during her readings and coaching sessions. She has helped thousands of people across the world build success in every area of their lives through her personal and group coaching, seminars and workshops, and her radio and television shows.

Anne is also the author of *Extreme Intuitive Makeover 55 Keys to Health, Wealth, and Happiness*, *Inner Visions The Healing Path of Art*, *Soul's Purpose Now Workbook*, *Spiritual Enlightenment Oracle Cards*, *A Toolkit for Creating Divine Magic and Miracles in Your Life*, creator of *Daily OM's Spend More Time Doing What You Love Online Course,* and a featured columnist on Beliefnet. Anne has published many self-help articles in magazines and online and is the host of *The Intuitive Millionaire Coach* television show. Her paintings are on display on the Laguna Beach Gallery CA website.

Please visit her website for your Prosperity Attraction Kit and a schedule of appearances at www.yourintuitivemakeover.com.